# RAISING A STRONG DAUGHTER

What Fathers Should

Know

Finlay Gow, JD and Kailin

Gow, MA

**Finlay Gow and Kailin Gow**

Raising a Strong Daughter:
What Fathers Should Know
Published by Sparklesoup Inc.
Copyright © 2018 Finlay Gow and Kailin
Gow

For information, please contact:

Sparklesoup Inc.
11700 W. Charleston Blvd. #170-95
Las Vegas, NV 89135
www.sparklesoup.com

# Raising A Strong Daughter

First Edition.
Printed in the United States of America.

## DEDICATION

To our fathers and grandfathers for instilling confidence in us and for going after their dreams whether it is to explore a new world, invent new inventions, start new businesses, go into politics, become an agent of change, or dare to be the caring father who took time out of their busy lives to make breakfast for us, take us fishing, teach us how to put together a business plan or even how

**Finlay Gow and Kailin Gow**

to be doting grandparents. Thank you for being there for us, always.

Raising A Strong Daughter

# TABLE OF CONTENT

Finlay Gow and Kailin Gow

## Raising Her to be a tougher target to would be attackers

## Raising Her how to handle safety in different situations

# INTRODUCTION

There are many books about parenting for women, but few books for men, when it comes to raising daughters. Yet there is a need for parents to help girls navigate through today's changing environment where women are now more active in all aspects of society and have assume roles other than the traditional roles for women in the past whether due to necessity or choice.

With women now assuming roles in politics, business, education, science and technology, arts, and even military; men's roles are changing as well.

**Finlay Gow and Kailin Gow**

Raising children, especially daughters, in today's world can be assumed by both parents, mothers, and fathers.

But when it comes to raising daughters, especially strong daughters, who will grow up to be strong women; fathers can and do play a very important role in their development and growth. Girls not only look to their mothers as role models of strength, but also their fathers. Men play an important role in helping the women and girls in their lives be empowered to be strong people who can pull their share of responsibilities, bring home the bacon (so to speak), take over the family business, and assume leadership positions. Just ask some of the women leaders profiled in some of the chapters in this book.

# A History of Strong Men Who Raised Strong Women

## Ancient Israel

The idea that women should be kept weak, uneducated, and dependent on a man in ancient civilization was somewhat misinterpreted and misused, if they were referring to biblical support. In fact, in Ancient Israel women could own property. The Book of Proverbs describes an ideal woman as a woman who has the means and capacity to make financial and business decisions. It says 'she considers a field and buys it'. (Proverbs 31:16)

Girls in Ancient Israel were taught valuable trade skills such as weaving, baking, and spinning to work and earn a living of their own.

## Ancient Greece

In Ancient Greece, women were expected to run businesses such as taverns, inns, and factories. They made and sold cloth, clothing, perfumes, farm equipment, and cooked food. Regardless of status and wealth. They were taught skills so they could survive on their own.

Girls were taught to read and write just as boys were, and women in wealthy families were expected to be well-educated.

Although they were not allowed to participate in the overall Olympic Games,

# Raising A Strong Daughter

they did have their own Women's Only Olympic Games dedicated to the goddess Hera (wife of Zeus). This was called The Heraean games which were held once every 4 years.

Women were even doctors, poets, and astronomers in Ancient Greece such as Metrodora was Greek woman doctor who lived in the 3rd or 4th century.

And of course, the women of Sparta were mothers, sisters, and daughters of Spartan warriors. They were expected to be just as tough. In fact, the women of Sparta were so revered by their husbands and fathers, mostly women were the landowners of Sparta.

## Ancient Rome

Women in Ancient Rome could own and inherit property as well as run businesses. Some women ran businesses in silver working and perfumery. Some women were priestesses or worked as midwives or hairdressers. And some women were gladiators.

## Ancient Egypt

In Ancient Greece, women held equal financial rights as men and were able to acquire, to own property in their own name as well as enter into contracts in their own name.

From Ancient times, women were recognized by law as being empowered to own property, run businesses, and handle their family's finances. The idea of

## Raising A Strong Daughter

coddling girls and not teaching them the same skills as their brothers did not appear to be from the ancient times.

In fact, the opposite was true. Girls were taught to be strong, capable, and empowered as boys in ancient laws and in the bible. So why is it somewhat a "new" concept of "strong" women today? No matter what the times, the responsibility to raise strong daughters is there. So in the following chapters, we have introduced some key secrets, written from a sociologist point of view, a lawyer's point of view, and also from the point of view of parents/uncles/aunts of girls.

**Finlay Gow and Kailin Gow**

# BUILDING SELF ESTEEM

It starts from the beginning.

The Webster dictionary defines self-esteem as:

*The holding a good opinion of one's self; self-complacency.*

Psychologists agree that having high self-esteem is one of the keys to success.

Why?

Having a high and good opinion of yourself matters more than how others think about you. To be able to bounce back and pick up yourself from obstacles in life, to be able to be unbreakable and strong, one must have high self-esteem.

An important part of parenting is developing your child's self-esteem. Raising your child to have a positive and resilient image of themselves can help them face challenges and overcome them. They will be able to say, "I am capable." And they will be able to feel "worthy".

Help build up your daughter's self-esteem to the point that no one could break it and she will always be able to stand confident and strong.

## Raising A Strong Daughter

There is the right way of building a person's self-esteem and a wrong way.

Simply telling your child she is great or wonderful or the prettiest or the best would only develop arrogance in her. They will grow pompous.

*Show* them instead how wonderful they are. Action speaks louder than words, and children are more perspective than we realize. They perceive action of their parents as being more truthful than spoken words. And they measure their self-worth based on how their parents act towards them.

Always show your words in action by following up what you say to her. For instance, when you tell your daughter, "You are so lovable," spend time with her to show she is lovable and worthy of spending time with.

Here are 4 short rules to remember when building your daughter's self-esteem:

1. Always tell her you love her. Demonstrate with hugs and kisses. Demonstrate with unconditional love.

2. Support them when they try new things. Encourage them so they are willing to go for things, to tackle new challenges.

3. Spend quality time with her. Be in the moment while you spend time with her and show her you enjoy it.

# Raising A Strong Daughter

4.  Don't compare her to others. By comparing her to others, you are signaling she is not good enough. She should be praise for her efforts and for her own accomplishments.

Finlay Gow and Kailin Gow

# Raising Her to Think For Herself

Your daughter does not have to be a lawyer in order to understand her rights. However, for her to be best equipped to defend herself and to protect herself, she should be armed with the knowledge of her rights.

Raising a daughter who is aware and knowledgeable of the world so that she can navigate through it with her eyes open, rather than closed, can be one of her best protection.

Knowledge is power.

## Raising A Strong Daughter

From the perspective of a woman who was and still is Daddy's little girl, I am grateful that my father never tried to shelter me or hide the truth of the world from me growing up. He included me in grown up conversations on what to do with the family business and even asked for my opinions.

From that alone, I felt like a valuable part of the family and that my thoughts and opinions mattered.

As a father, you can validate your daughter's thoughts and opinions by asking for them and listening to her. You can build up her confidence in her thinking abilities by showing her that her thoughts are thoughtful and legitimate.

And if her opinions and thinking is valid, then praise her for coming up with valid and good ideas.

Some fathers whose daughters have grown up to become lawyers, judges, executives, senators, and even Presidents (Taiwan's president is a woman lawyer), even made it a point to teach or guide their daughters in the skill of negotiations and debate.

It can start at the youngest of age when babies are taught that if they ask for something, they are rewarded. Or later as toddlers, when they learn to use the magic words, "Pretty please."

To build up negotiation and thinking skills, you can practice setting rules with

## Raising A Strong Daughter

your daughter and if she wants to bend the rules, to have her come up with a "what if I do my chores earlier so I can play video games for an extra hour" kind of negotiations.

Lawyer and host Kimberley Guilfoyle credits her father for helping her become the woman she is when she says, "He was the best coach in my life. I was a little shy and introverted, and he wanted me to be the woman who would stand on her own two feet and have the self-esteem and stand for myself, no matter what."

Be the best coach for your daughter by guiding her to think for herself.

# RAISING HER TO BE RESOURCEFUL

When you think of someone who is resourceful, you may picture a man who is able to build a boat out of duct tape or a MacGyver-type of person who can figure out a way out of any close quarters.

Even the image of a cool-headed super spy like James Bond may come to mind.

Now picture your daughter being able to figure out a way out of tough situations, able to solve problems that may

# Raising A Strong Daughter

face in school and/or in the workplace. She may not need to be a MacGyver or a James Bond, but she would still need the same kind of skills to help her navigate through everyday life.

Entrepreneurs and resilient people are resourceful. Some may call them "scrappy" or "inventive" or even "enterprising".

When it comes to finding a solution, they may get creative. To think out of the box, sometimes, being creative would mean to bend the rules.

In order to be successful as a woman, teach your daughter to never apologize for her success. Men never have to apologize for it, why should the women who earned it?

Raise your daughter to be adaptable. Resourceful people can adapt and change directions to fit the situation. Being able to adapt and change is a strength that has allowed humankind to flourish throughout civilization. For your daughter to survive and flourish in a changing environment, she should learn to be flexible, adaptable, and teachable.

Resourceful people also are adaptable to more than one plan in case one does not work out.

Teach your daughter to rely on people as resources so she can get the help she needs when she needs it. Forming friendships, relationships with mentors and teachers, classmates and co-workers and even a significant other who can support,

26

## Raising A Strong Daughter

encourage, and help her when she needs help is important in establishing a strong center of resources she can count on for any situation.

In line with that, teach and guide your daughter to be able to assert herself and ask for what they need. Being able to ask is one of the biggest skills and positive attitudes that can propel your daughter into success.

And lastly, teach your daughter to be able to use what technologies are available and the tools around her. Technology is meant to help improve human lives. There are many out there and several new innovations that can help a person become more productive, see and do things beyond our human abilities, and more. By mastering the use of these technologies, your daughter would be a far stronger person overall.

# RAISING HER TO BE INDEPENDENT

There isn't a magic formula for teaching someone to become independent. A person becomes independent when they are no longer a dependent.

By law, minors become independent when they are of age. The age of adulthood varies from country to country and even from state to state.

It is assumed that a person is capable of acting and thinking as an adult when they become of age.

## Finlay Gow and Kailin Gow

To best prepare your daughter to become a strong and independent person would be to raise her the best you can so she can be able to *do* things for herself. That she can be able to live on her own. That she can be able to take care of her own finances, her own household...basically her own life.

Raising her to be independent is to raise her to become a fully functioning and productive adult in society.

Most of the time, it happens without us parents even consciously trying. That is because throughout our children's lives, they are learning and striving to become an independent adult. All their lives as children, they are learning how to be an adult person through everything they see, observe, study, experience, sense, and take

# Raising A Strong Daughter

in, especially through the adults around them.

So that means, as the adults closest to them, your daughter is learning to be more like you or to learn to be more like the grownups they have around them. You, grandparents, uncles, aunts, teachers, guardians, their friends' parents, and your grown friends.

Be the kind of person you want your daughter to marry. Help and empower your spouse to be the strong independent and happy fulfilled person you want your daughter to be like. Teach and guide your sons to be the kind of men who would stand up for and protect their sisters so their sisters would know and choose to marry men who protect and treat the women in their lives with love and respect.

Surround yourself with friends and grownups who are respectful to women.

And for practical matters, there are 10 life skills your child, especially during their teen years should learn:

1) Interpersonal Skills
2) Goal setting and Resourcefulness Skills
3) Time management Skills
4) Money management Skills
5) Ability to Find Housing
6) Ability to Drive or Obtain Transportation
7) Ability to Obtain and/or Cook Food

# Raising A Strong Daughter

8) General Housekeeping Skills
9) Ability to Obtain and Keep a Job
10) Ability to Cope with Loneliness

## Interpersonal Skills

Interpersonal skills not only include making and keeping friends, but how to get along well with others in the workplace, how to have a long-lasting relationship with a significant other, and even the daily interaction one has with people from all walks of life.

## Goal setting and Resourcefulness Skills

Help and guide your daughter to define her goals in life and how to obtain them. Build her confidence and self-esteem up with goals she can easily obtain first to show her how.

33

For example, if her goal is to bake a birthday cake for Mommy, then help her figure out how such as help her bake the cake by reading a cookbook together, by watching a baking video together, or by enrolling her in a kids baking class.

Little by little, by setting small goals and accomplishing them, she is learning how to work towards and earning her accomplishments through setting a goal and figuring out a way to accomplish it.

## Time Management Skills

Teach your daughter time management skills which would help her become a well-balanced, productive, and happier person. Here are some ways to manage time more efficiently:

34

# Raising A Strong Daughter

1) Prioritize.

   Choose to pay attention to the most important activities and relationships. Then set a plan for your week.

2. Learn when to say NO.

There are always things we have to do. But being able to choose which things to do and saying NO to other things instead of everything, can help life be more manageable.

3. Set a Time Limit to activities that Consume All Your Time.

For example, if your daughter is spending all her time watching videos instead of other things, limit her video watching time. Help her set her time limit to those activities by helping her set her schedule and put her in charge of managing her own schedule.

1. Schedule In Your 'Do Not Disturb' Time.

   Block out time in your schedule to work on projects that require more focus. Then turn off devices, put up signs "Do Not Disturb" or wear a noise-blocking headphone (helpful in dorms or with roommates) to help you concentrate.

# Raising A Strong Daughter

2. To Help You Focus and Save Time, Reduce stress.

   Encourage your daughter to remember to keep herself healthy by eating nutritious foods, exercising, sleeping enough, and resting.

## Money management Skills

Managing money is a life-long skill that empowers your daughter to be able to have more control and freedom over her life.

Teaching her about money and its ability to provide people with choices and opportunities empowers her to manage money more wisely. Empower her to learn to earn, save, and invest money wisely will help her have more security and independence in her life.

From an early age, children can be taught about money by recognizing how to use it as they observe how parents use it when buying groceries, goods, or services.

Include your daughter in discussions of money;  take her along on shopping trips or to restaurants or other places to observe how the exchange of money is an everyday occurrence in society.

Give your daughter an allowance when she is younger so she can learn to save or spend her money by managing her allowance budget.

When she is older as a teen, give her a clothing budget or a budget on things she enjoys so she will be able to have the freedom to choose what to spend her money on, but also figure out how to manage what she has.

## Ability to Find Housing

For the daughter who has already or is about to go to college or move out on her own, help her understand the finances of finding a place to live. Help her to be able to research and find the safest and best neighborhoods for her to live in. If rent is beyond her means, help her to be able to find roommates or an affordable place that is still safer. Help her determine whether it would be better to live close to school or work or whether it would be better to commute further.

## Ability to Drive or Obtain Transportation

Teach your daughter how to drive safely or have her learn it through a driving school. The ability to have your own transportation is one of the most useful tools to have in empowering your daughter.

The next best thing is to teach her how to obtain transportation either through public transportation, her friends or friends' parents or through private transportation (taxi, private car). Teach her how to spot safe vehicles, how to take down the taxi or private car's information, and how to be an informed and aware passenger.

## Ability to Obtain and/or Cook Food

# Raising A Strong Daughter

Today there are many ways to learn how to cook. There are cooking classes offered through community courses, online, through grocery stores or specialty stores or restaurants, and even cooking schools. There are also well-written easy-to-follow cookbooks that can instruct people how to cook.

Even better is when a parent or relative teaches a child how to cook, especially family recipes that should be pass down from generation after generation. If you are fortunate enough to be a good cook or your spouse or parent is, then teach your child some cooking skills enough for them to be able to prepare their own meals.

And your child should learn how to obtain, buy, and order food on their own.

You can practice having them order their own food at restaurants, shop for groceries at markets, and even learn to grow food in a garden or in potted plants.

## General Housekeeping Skills

Knowing how to do basic housekeeping is important in how to maintain their own housing so doing the laundry, cleaning their room, loading/unloading the dishwasher, taking out the trash can help them learn to do general housekeeping when they move out on their own.

## Ability to Obtain and Keep a Job

To live on her own independently, your daughter should be able to obtain a job that earns enough to pay for her expenses.

42

## Raising A Strong Daughter

To help her learn to get a job, help your daughter learn how to interview for a job. Instill in her a hard work ethic and the pride of doing her job well.

Raise your daughter to be dependable, reliable, and a team player.

Raise her to be competent, sensible, fair, and someone who is trustworthy.

## **Ability to Cope with Loneliness**

Independence gives freedom, but it also means that for one to stand on their own, they will have to stand alone...for a while. Teach your daughter that loneliness is temporary, and can be coped with through her social circle and support group, which definitely should include you.

Finlay Gow and Kailin Gow

# Raising Her to handle harassment

As a parent, it's difficult to fathom
that your child will, with almost a certainty,
be subjected to adult problems like sexual
harassment. The thought is appalling and
horrific, and like most fathers, we will do
anything to protect our children. Talk to any
father, and they shudder at the thought of
their child being harassed. Moreover, such
talk evokes anger and a sudden willingness
to commit untoward acts against
perpetrators. Nevertheless, a certain
segment of society still accepts the notion
that "boys will be boys" and tolerates (if not
perpetuates) a certain aggressiveness toward

# Raising A Strong Daughter

the opposite sex. Clearly, boundaries must be drawn and in general, they are – in the form of harassment laws.

A security expert once told me that locks and alarms are great, but they only work for a law-abiding people. A criminal will break through a door if he really wants to enter a building, regardless what obstacles you put in front of him. That being said, common sense tells us that laws only apply to law-abiding people, and in the world of sexual harassment, I venture to say that most people do not know the law, and even if they do, they tend to interpret the law in a light most permissive to their own actions and beliefs.

That being said, what are the laws governing sexual harassment? Well, the answer isn't quite as simple as one would think, as it requires break down into civil and criminal law components. This is not intended to be a comprehensive discussion of the topic, but a general overview, as I would not be able to do justice on a topic that would span across multiple shelves at the Library of Congress.

First, let's look at laws in the general context. Simply by being a member of society, you have a fundamental right to be left alone. Don't bug me and I won't bug you. Nevertheless, some people will bug you and some won't mind their own business. Worse, some will invade your personal space, and go as far as saying bad things or even making unwanted physical contact. Obviously, society can't function if we disallowed all forms of intentional

# Raising A Strong Daughter

interaction, but therein serves the function so laws, to act as guidelines for acceptable behavior. Invade someone's space, and you might commit a tort for assault. If you strike a person, it becomes a tortious battery. If you do something worse, it becomes criminal. Make unwanted sexual advances, commit sexual harassment. The discussion here isn't just about sexual harassment, it's about how to teach my daughter on how to avoid the problem, and how to deal with it if it can't be avoided.

But laws only affect law abiding people. You can discourage someone from breaking the law, but you can't stop someone who is hell bent on doing whatever bad acts they intend to commit.

Here's what I tell my child. Avoid problems before they start. They say that success leaves clues and I feel that Problems are the same way. Most of them can be avoided. Whether it is harassment, unwanted attention, or otherwise, there are ways to minimize problems in your life.

*Be observant*. There are good and bad people in this world. Why, she asks? I have no good answer to this question, but I have a theory. People aren't all brought up the same way, and they have different perspectives on what is right and wrong. That being the case, you can't assume anything about anyone without having some concrete basis to make a determination. Observe their mannerisms, how they care for themselves, how they treat you, how they treat others, how they treat their pets,

# Raising A Strong Daughter

etc. One of the most important skills you can learn is to stop and observe. Carefully. When she was 10, I sat inside the car at a gas station and told her to observe all of the people going in and out of the convenience store. Look at their body language, look at their faces, their hands, their movements. Everyone has a story, and without hearing them or speaking with them, you can get a good idea about what they are doing. Ask any law enforcement professional and they will tell you that observing a person's eyes and their hands will tell you a lot about the nature of their business. The simple skill of observation will go a long way toward avoiding trouble. As they say, God gave you two eyes and two ears and only one mouth. Watch, listen, and observe before you speak or engage. Trouble will find you, but if you find trouble first, you are well ahead of the game. Avoid trouble whenever possible. Avoid sketchy people, sketchy places, and the unknown. You will have enough problems in life, no point in attracting problems or finding yourself in the middle of something that complicates your existence.

*Trust but Verify*. As many people will profess, I am a walking advice machine. I've told countless people that about the old Ronald Reagan adage, trust but verify. For those of you who are older, you will understand what I'm getting at. The older you get, the more you understand this notion. Over time, you encounter enough people in your life to understand that some people are trustworthy, some are untrustworthy, and some you simply need more time or interaction before you can cast

# Raising A Strong Daughter

judgment. Ultimately, they all fall into one of two camps. And until you can trust them, trust is always provisional and temporary. Even a best friend can turn into an enemy in a heartbeat. I don't intend to be cynical, but trust is something that can take a lifetime to earn, and split second to lose. And it is almost impossible to earn back. So I explain to all of this to my young daughter at an early age and she has no idea what I'm talking about. But I repeat the line like a broken record and it sinks in more and more. I give this advice to people throughout their 20s and 30s and the come back to thank me for the words of wisdom. How do you avoid harassment? Don't hang around people who aren't trustworthy. That could be in the form of respect, honesty, or politeness. Spot these traits, or the absence thereof, and you are on your wage to avoiding problems.

Start hanging around people with these traits (or hanging around people who associate with bad people), and trouble will surely find you.

*Seek assistance*.  Try as you might to avoid problems, every once in a while, some problems latch onto you and they won't relent.   I assure my daughter that I will always be there for her.   If she does something bad, she can count on me to be there to assist her.  She has to own up to her own responsibility, but I am always going to be looking out for her best interest.  Nobody in the world will defend her more fiercely. Nobody.  As dads can relate, you will jump in front of a speeding locomotive if you knew it would save your child's life. Naturally, you can't coddle a kid and protecting from everything.  That wouldn't

# Raising A Strong Daughter

be good for them. A life without adversity is a life that avoids reality. Kids need to experience adversity in order to understand problems, evaluate solutions, and take appropriate action. But you aren't alone in the world. Talk to smart people with good judgment. Talk to someone with authority whose responsibility is to remedy problems. Talk to law enforcement. Use common sense. And by golly, avoid listening to idiots who try to pass themselves off as smart people with good judgment. As I said earlier, success leaves clues. If you have a hard time screening out good versus bad advice, lean toward those who have a successful tract record. But as a dad, don't assume that you know everything. If you are ignorant, recognize your limitations and seek out advice for yourself before you become the idiot giving bad advice.

*Defend yourself.* After everything is said and done, we can't be everywhere for our daughters. You hope to raise them with healthy, positive experiences, and a strong sense of right and wrong, just and unjust, moral and immoral. And when being observant, discerning who to trust or distrust, and seeking out help fails to avoid the problem at hand, our daughter needs to know how to defend herself. Not simply in the physical sense, but in the emotional sense as well. A strong, healthy self-esteem will do wonders to fend off attack from mean girls, mean boys, or even unnamed faceless trolls on social media. My daughter has always been reassured that she is smart and capable, but that does not excuse continuous learning. She has been assured that she is pretty, but that does not excuse

# Raising A Strong Daughter

healthy habits. She has been assured that she is gifted, but those gifts evolve and she will continue to discover more of them as she grows older, and those gifts must be put to good use. My daughter has no peer pressure issues. If she doesn't like something, nobody is telling her how to think. She cooperates, but sometimes under protest. She will grow to be a strong healthy spirited child emotionally because her parents love her, but continuously work to give her the kinds of well rounded experiences that help her adapt to the things she will encounter as an adult. At the same time, if she faces physical danger, she has the fundamental right to defend herself. Self defense is important for young girls and adults, and it is not to be taken for granted. In most cases, victims were easy targets. Harden targets are those who are observant, avoid questionable people and situations, and who physically fight back. With proper supervision and guidance, I will give my daughter the tools to defend herself and her loved ones. The world is a tough place and again, we can't be there throughout every moment of their lives. My daughter isn't going to grow up as fragile flower, incapable of taking care of herself. She will train as she fights, and she will fight as she trains. She will be raised to be total bad ass. Because everyone loves a bad ass. Just ask Lara Croft.

Let's shift over to a discussion about laws in the workplace. Anti-harassment laws can vary from state to state, city to city, and even company to company. Different companies have different tolerance levels for bad behavior, and generally handle conflicts differently, with some being much more lenient than others. There is a fundamental obligation for employers to prevent harassment of any type in the workplace. We all go to work for a purpose, and generally that is to serve a function that provides some level of utility to the employer. Being harassed isn't usually part of that equation (although it seems there are always exceptions to every rule). Accordingly, employers are tasked with preventing workplace harassment, stopping harassment when it occurs, and preventing any type of predictable reoccurrence. So the situation will dictate what actions must be taken and there are far too many instances to explain how to go about preventing or fixing every problem. But on the topic of harassment, it usually starts with one individual being attracted to another individual. And when that attraction isn't mutual, it can devolve from there, where the balance shifts from tolerable

As a corporate lawyer for some very large, notable corporations, I've seen a broad spectrum of bad behavior. In fact, I've seen so much bad behavior, I'd like to believe that I can predict behavior based on job position and personality traits. I don't intend to overstate my abilities, but my experience comes from having worked at companies with hundreds of thousands of employees, where I dealt with their issues day in and day out for nearly two decades. After a while, you feel like you've heard everything. So when I say that behavior is predictable, it does fall into patterns of opportunity, and the outcome and remedy is always where I start my analysis.

# Raising A Strong Daughter

Workplace harassment is the stuff that makes the news. It involves high dollars when applied to large corporations. It can be salacious and titillating, giving rise to best selling novels and movies made for television. In truth, it happens a lot less than you'd think, and quite frankly, mostly a function of individual sensitivities, miscommunication between parties, and a misunderstanding of individual points of view.

Without going in depth into the laws about sexual harassment in particular, California's Department of Fair Employment and Housing provides the following definition:

**Finlay Gow and Kailin Gow**

*State regulations define sexual harassment as unwanted sexual advances, or visual, verbal or physical conduct of a sexual nature. It includes many forms of offensive behavior and includes gender-based harassment of a person of the same sex as the harasser. The following is a partial list of prohibited behavior:*

- *Visual conduct: leering, making sexual gestures, displaying of sexually suggestive objects or pictures, cartoons or posters.*

- *Verbal conduct: making or using derogatory comments, epithets, slurs and jokes. Verbal abuse of a sexual nature, graphic verbal commentaries*

60

# Raising A Strong Daughter

*about an individual's body, sexually degrading words used to describe an individual.*

- *Physical conduct: touching, assault, impeding or blocking movements.*

- *Offering employment benefits in exchange for sexual favors.*

- *Making or threatening retaliatory action after receiving a negative response to sexual advances.*

There are two basic types of sexual harassment violations in the workplace. The first is *Quid Pro Quo* sexual harassment, where a supervisor conditions receiving some employment benefit upon an employee agreeing to a sexual demand. Typically, it involves things like offering of a favorable performance review, a promotion, a pay raise, or a preferential job assignment in exchange for sexual favors. This type of sexual harassment is treated very harshly under the law, imposing strict liability (meaning no excuses) upon an employer whose supervisory personnel commits such a violation. The second type of harassment is characterized as a *Hostile Work Environment* where: (1) enduring offensive conduct becomes a condition of continued employment, or (2) offensive conduct is severe or pervasive enough to create a work

# Raising A Strong Daughter

environment that a reasonable person would consider it to be intimidating, hostile, or abusive. While hostile work environment is not always sexual in nature, it creates potential liability for an employer whenever the employer is given awareness of a situation, and then fails to mitigate or remedy the problem.

Again, this discussion isn't about sexual harassment itself, but what a father can teach his daughter about working and surviving in a workplace. It isn't an easy task trying to teach a child on how to deal with adult problems, but we should teach them what work is all about at an early age. Kids understand that dad goes to work, but do they really know how a person earns his or her pay? I'm a fan of Take Your Child to Work days, but it starts with a simple discussion about capitalism and earning your wages by providing beneficial services to someone who needs it. You aren't entitled to anything in life, except the pursuant of life, liberty, and happiness. But life isn't easy and outside a parent's unconditional love, nothing is actually free. Once the foundation is set, we talk about how people come together in an office and work together. That's why team work is important. I can't say that no person is island because some people are quite effective working alone. However, working as a team is almost always a better option – when it is an option. Let me get to the point, what do you tell your daughter about working outside, and avoiding workplace harassment? As I said before, laws only apply to law-abiding people. And some people are incorrigible.

# Raising A Strong Daughter

*Avoidance*.  As previously discussed, the best way to avoid a problem is to identify its source and curtail your exposure to the risk. If there are creeps at work, avoid them.  Put people in between you and those people. Don't hang around them or the places where they frequent.  If they follow you, be in places where you will have supervisors present.  Report your issues to friends and supervisors. Supervisors have a duty to protect against harassment in the workplace.

*Never give them an excuse*.  I will say it because it is basically true.  Men are incorrigible and look for opportunities.  If you flirt with a man, you give him hope.  If you don't flirt with a man, you still give him false hope.  If you turn him down, he will still have hope. If you are nice and polite, he will see this as an invitation. If you kick him in the groin, he will still think there is a chance because you did not kill him. It's like the Jim Carrey scene in Dumb and Dumber, even when he was told he had a one in a million chance with a girl, he still understood it to mean he had a chance. Men need to be told both physically and personally and you can't really be too blunt about it. Be diplomatic, but blunt. And make sure you have people to watch your back, which gets to the next point.

*Diplomacy and Politics*. In life, the mere fact that you must work with human beings generates political considerations. When I say "politics," I am not referring to governmental politics, but the interaction between human beings and their emotions. Put two people together in a room and you

# Raising A Strong Daughter

usually don't have any politics. Put three people together and instantly there will be politics with each person having a certain set of interests and desired outcomes. Each will work strategically to improve their situation and maximize their chances to obtain a particular result. So I tell my daughter that people need to work together, but always try to understand your priorities, and the priorities of *others*. In most cases, your priority is not the same as theirs, and to get their help, you need to understand what their interests are. Only then can you devise a pathway to get them to help you on your priorities. In this exchange, you will maximize the chance for a favorable outcome. When you play your politics right, you create allies, and allies help each other in times of need. Being political savvy can be one of your greatest tools to get out of problems.

*There is no such thing as a free lunch*. Recognizing that everything comes at a price is important. I've explained the concept of politics with my daughter and while benevolence does exist, there is always an underlying motive. People will be attracted to do you and with that interaction, you may or may not share the attraction. Ignorance is bliss, but it can be foolhardy. Be mindful of people's motives with everything you do, or everything that is done for you. Don't be paranoid, just be mindful.

*See something, Say something*. An important principle in law and in life. Your first obligation is to protect yourself. If you

# Raising A Strong Daughter

don't agree with something, don't be afraid to say no. Never be afraid to say no. Be diplomatic, but no means no. And if you are required to escalate that no, then do it. If you need allies, then use your friends and political influences. The first step in addressing a harassment problem is to tell someone to stop. Document it, have witnesses, make the issue known to friends and supervisors. Say no more than once. People fear retribution, but truth be told, no job is worth harassment. And the law will protect you against retaliation because it is illegal for employers to punish you for exercising your rights.

*Investigation and Resolution*.  By law, employers are required to investigate bona fide complaints. Be sure to complain when you have problems. Failure to complain not only results in continuing the problem, but allowing the problem to affect others as well. Never feel guilt over problems you didn't start. Accountability is important in life because without it, you have anarchy.

As I started, this is a very tough area to talk about with a child. The subject matter involves adult problems, and kids don't understand adult problems. But by breaking it down piece by piece, and component by component, kids can learn how to develop fundamental skills that they don't teach in school. Kids will surprise you. They are smarter than you think, more capable than society wants to believe, and often see things with greater clarity than adults. I'm not training my daughter to deal with sexual harassment specifically, I'm giving her tools with global, life long application. The best

## Raising A Strong Daughter

thing we can do for our kids is prepare them to handle problems. Identifying those problems in advance and working through their solutions is important early on in life. When she encounters these problems in the future, it will not be the first time she has ever faced these issues, and she stands a better chance of handling the situation successfully.

# Raising her to know how to fight

This chapter is literally about fighting. A strong girl no matter how girly she is, whether she loves unicorns and rabbits and wear sparkly stars in her hair and glitter nail polish, needs to know how to defend herself.

As a parent, you would do anything to protect your child. You would try to always be there for her. However, it is not realistic to always be there for her 24/7. Raise your daughter so she is not a damsel in distress. Raise her so she can be the one saving herself. This doesn't mean that she

# Raising A Strong Daughter

would be less feminine or girly if she knows how to fight. It means she can be herself, and she can protect herself, too. So raise your child to learn how to protect themselves.

80% of sexual assaults may be preventable by applying crime prevention precautions. Think that if more people, especially your daughters, wives, sisters, and mothers knew what to do to prevent crime by taking precautions, then that 80% would decrease.

There are self-defense classes for women and teens offered through community programs, videos, and online. There are also martial arts and boxing classes for women, teens, and children offered everywhere.

The key to learning self-defense and other martial arts movements is practice. Whatever type of self-defense and fighting styles your daughter learns, instilling the movements and techniques used to fight back against an assailant should be practiced so often that it becomes intuitive and ingrained in her.

Like riding a bicycle, becoming proficient and even very good at self-defense and martial arts takes commitment and practice. Treat it like a sport which your daughter grows better with practice. A swimmer swims; an artist paints; so must an independent strong woman practice and gain the skills to defend herself.

Although guns have become a controversial topic and political debate

74

# Raising A Strong Daughter

recently, and regardless of your opinion on guns, the fact remains that the majority of students and people training to become Concealed weapons holders are women and the elderly.

Why?

Knowing how to use a firearm to protect and prevent an attack can level the field for those not physically intimidating or as strong as the attacker. Women and the elderly are in general, physically smaller and has less strength than men. It is a generalization based on science. So it is most likely a would-be attacker would be someone who is physically larger and stronger than a woman or elderly person.

Using a firearm responsibly and correctly takes practice. Knowing the rules of owning and using a firearm in the form of a Concealed Weapons permit requires training, practice, and testing.

## RAISING HER TO BE A TOUGHER TARGET TO WOULD BE ATTACKERS

## Getting Back to Our Innate Sense of Awareness

To be a strong independent woman or person, your daughter must understand that personal security is her own responsibility and cannot be delegated to others.

To be able to best handle personal security in any situation, she must first develop a keen sense of awareness and an attitude of toughness that makes her a tough target to potential attackers.

Because the world is constantly changing and safety cannot be guaranteed, developing a keen awareness helps her assess danger and risks. In nature, awareness and assessment of danger is almost instinctual. Animals seem to be born aware of danger and their environment. Yet as humans, living in the city or in a community dependent on others for safety; we lost this instinctual awareness of danger. And what is amazing in nature is that the female, because of their role to protect their young and to protect their family or social group, are the ones with the keener sense of awareness. Yet this is the opposite with humans where the females are less aware of

# Raising A Strong Daughter

danger and less able to personally defend and protect themselves as well as their young. So, raise your daughter to change this so her innate sense of awareness is developed as it should be.

As in nature, you want to be the tough target. You want to make it as hard as possible for potential attackers to attack you. A person who is a tougher target for attackers is someone who accepts that there is danger in our world. That people can be vulnerable. Despite our vulnerabilities, a tougher target builds up their strengths to compensate for the vulnerabilities. It is not just about buying and carrying a personal safety device or weapon. It is about the awareness and ability of how and when to use them correctly.

Developing a keen awareness is developing an overall attitude towards our everyday living and by knowing there are potential danger in it.

Be proactive in protecting yourself. By being aware, you can apply proactive protection techniques to deter and even get the criminal/attacker arrested and confined. Here are 4 strategies to be proactive in protecting yourself:

1. Reduce the value of the reward in the criminal's mind.
2. Remove and lessen any excuses a criminal has in approaching you and/or your property.
3. Make it as hard as possible for the criminal to commit the crime.
4. Make it known and clear to potential offender that he might be harmed

and/or apprehended if he intends on targeting you or your property.

When she develops a keen awareness, she can apply the anti-terrorism doctrine below:

- DETECT the threat
- DETER the threat
- DENY access to the threat
- DELAY the attack if possible

**Using Technology for Defense**

Technological defenses can be used to detect danger, delay danger, and deter danger.

They can be devices such as cameras, wired fences, walls, automatic lighting systems, alarm systems, locks, sirens, tasers, and sound systems. Use technology to layer on defenses instead of relying on it as a sole defense. Criminals may bypass your defenses including your technological defenses so be prepare with learned fighting techniques and skills to combat this possibility.

## Using Personal Safety Devices

Because an attacker may not know you are armed or he intends to neutralize it, having a weapon or gadget for self-defense does not lower the chance of attack or improve your personal safety.

However, it can be for self-protection successfully for self-protection when used properly and in favorable conditions.

# Raising A Strong Daughter

Here are Possible Self-Protection Items That Can Be used Successfully *When they are Delivered with Force at a Vulnerable Part of an Assailant's Body*:

- Rock
- Stick
- Tools
- Kitchen Utensils
- Household Items
- Hammers
- Screw drivers
- Bug Sprays
- Keys
- Books
- Cups
- Pens
- Pepper Sprayers
- Tasers
- Firearms

Weapons and personal safety devices can be a handicap when you don't know how to use it properly, and it can be used against you. For instance when you have to use valuable time to find or take out your selected device in your hand and it get ready. Or if it was taken away or it malfunctions.

To use your devices properly, you have to practice and train to use them; and learn self-defense without using a personal safety device in addition to having a personal safety device.

# RAISING HER HOW TO HANDLE SAFETY IN DIFFERENT SITUATIONS

## Crime within Relationships

This is the most common threat to personal safety and healthy well-being. Battery, burglary, especially sexual assault are most often committed by someone the victim are acquainted with and knows.

And the victims of physical violence within relationships tend to be mostly females, however boys can be victimized and abused by both male and female abusers.

The sad part is in addition to being abused, abused children tend to have a higher tendency to become abusive toward others, especially those whom they know.

## Raise Your Daughter to Avoid an Abusive Personality

Part of life and growing up is the selection of a mate. You want your daughter to find and be in a healthy relationship that is built on mutual trust.

The first line of defense for a life of heartache and abuse because of an abusive relationship, is to help your daughter be aware of and to avoid a potential mate with an abusive personality.

# Raising A Strong Daughter

Abusive personalities who become attached to your daughter can do enormous damage to her emotionally, physically, and mentally. Living with an abusive personality can be debilitating, as well as eroding to a person's self-esteem, confidence, strength, and health.

Help your daughter be aware of the traits of an abusive personality which are the following:

## 1. Low Self-Esteem

- Has a poor opinion of himself and often mask or conceal his low self-esteem in defensive, projecting, and assaultive behavior.

- Degrades and criticizes others to appear superior and compensate for low self-esteem.
- Belief that he is a perpetual failure.
- Feels worthlessness and unlovable.
- Turns attention to himself when his partner is upset and in need of comfort or support.
- Seeks to make his partner feel bad so they can feel better about himself.
- Requires his ego be constantly confirmed and needs to be told how great he is.
- Explosive reactions to stress.
- Has mood swings.

# Raising A Strong Daughter

- Seeks control by controlling his partner.
- Doesn't have close friends
- Talks about grand ambitions but does not initiate actions toward goals.
- Lazy and freeloading
- Resents the people he is dependent upon.

## 2. Feelings are Moody and Cyclical

- uncomfortable when things are going well in a relationship.
- Cannot accept rejection.
- Blames others for his feelings.
- Manipulates his partner through her feelings

- Belittles his partner's feelings
- Explosive temper
- Breaks things

## 3. History of Abuse within Relationships

- Was abused and/or neglected as a child.
- Has stalked previous partners.
- Discusses abuse and neglect during his childhood upbringing.
- Was sexually abused or shamed by a male or female caregiver, or authority figure.

While 1/3 of abused children repeat the abuse as an adult, 2/3 of abused children do

Raising A Strong Daughter

not repeat the cycle they witnessed so it shows the majority of abused children overcome the abuse and go on to live a healthy and productive life.

**4. Views Women with Fear and Disrespect**

- Degrade women with comments about their bodies
- Compares his partner to other women's bodies and behavior
- Tells his partner she is there to serve him or other men.
- Tells his partner he sexually owns her.
- Idolizes his partner on a pedestal but knocks her down take down her self-esteem.

- Accuses his partner of trying to control him.
- Withhold love, approval, affection and appreciation to his partner to punish her.
- Calls and refers to women in derogatory names and terms.

## 5. Overly Possessive Jealousy

## 6. Substance Abuse

## 7. Financial Problems

- Can't keep a job
- Feels threatened by other people's success
- Refuses to let his partner work outside the home.

- Causes problems for his partner at work, and sometimes gets her fired.
- Conceals financial information from his partner.
- Tells his partner to turn over her money to him.
- Controls his partner's finances until she is dependent on him.

## 8. Conflict

- Charming in public and with acquaintances, but is degrading and mean to his partner and family members in private.

- Resolves conflict through aggressiveness, intimidation, bullying, and violence.
- Is verbally abusive.
- Controls his partner's attire
- Withholds food and medicine to his partner.
- Convinces his partner's friends, children, and family into believing she is psychologically unbalanced, or "crazy".
- Uses children as pawns to manipulate and control his partner.

Raising A Strong Daughter

# Helping Your Daughter End an Abusive Relationship

Your daughter will need your help in ending an abusive relationship. Often heightened awareness and additional personal safety will be needed when ending a bad dating relationship or abusive marriage especially with abusive personalities that can lead to stalking.

# Raise Your Daughter to Handle Bullying

Crimes in relationship also include bullying, especially in the workplace. Bullying can be intrusive in a work environment, negatively impacting the safety and work conditions of employment.

Bullying in school should not be tolerated. If your daughter faces instances of bullying, she should approach her teacher, school administrators, and/or someone of authority to report it.

Fear of retaliation may cause her to not report bullying, but the fear of further bullying should be out weigh retaliation. Reporting the bullying incidence will put it on record. With reported incidences, you are building up your arsenal against the bully and signaling that their behavior was not consensual and welcome.

# Defending Against a Date Rapist

## Date Rapists Are Acquaintance Rapists

An acquaintance rapist is someone the victim knows such as a family member, friend, co-worker, fellow student, neighbor, or a date.

All rapists are predators and low life wolves, but the acquaintance rapist is one who appears as a friend wearing the sheep's clothing but is waiting for a chance to lure their victims into isolation.

They often have abusive personalities and have no boundaries. They are amoral and feel no remorse for the crimes they commit.

What sets them apart from any acquaintance or potential dating partner is their abusive personalities, inability to accept rejection and the word "no", is persistent in pushing the girl to date him or for sex even when she is uncomfortable with him, he knows too much about her often without her divulging the information (i.e. a creep), and he keeps wanting to get her alone with him.

If your daughter comes across someone like this, tell her it is time to create distance and safety from him.

Recognizing the behavioral traits of the date rapist and acquaintance rapist

# Raising A Strong Daughter

important   to   help   avoid   crimes   in
relationships.

# Stalking

## What Is Stalking?

Stalking is defined as a behavior composed of a series of acts over a period of time, however short, but with an intended purpose of harassment and intimidation.

It is similar to hunting where a predator is hunting its prey.

It is a crime of relationship that involves multiple or continue acts of repeated victimization, even if the relationship exists only in the predator's mind.

# Raising A Strong Daughter

Black's Law Dictionary (2012) describes stalking as: "The offense of following or loitering near another, often surreptitiously, to annoy or harass that person or to commit a further crime such as assault or battery.

Stalking can be a terrifying experience for victims and their families. It is intrusive violation of privacy with the constant fear of potentially being physically harmed or killed, or the constant anxiety that a loved one may be harmed.

## Defending Against Stalkers

- Approach the problem with several methods of threat management all at the same time such as:

- improve physical home security
- Take financial protective measures
- Seek aid from others
- Note repeated notifications and reminders regarding the threat
- Take personal securities
- Take self-defense classes
- Add surveillance
- Obtain a restraining order
- Get counseling or therapy

Raising A Strong Daughter

# Avoid Dating Violence by Preparing Before Dating

Avoid potential dating violence by doing your research and preparing before dating.

## How to Prepare Before Date

- Avoid pity dates
- Take responsibility for your safety.
- Do not accept the date if you feel uncomfortable
- Know your boundaries and limitations.
- Set firm ground rules.

- Let someone else know about your plans and destination.
- Select a safe meeting location.
- Have a plan on how to get home.
- Know yourself so you won't be manipulated into something you don't want to do.

Don't interact with someone who makes you feel uncomfortable.

## During the Date

- Don't rely on pepper spray and other gadgets or weapons for self-defense.

## Raising A Strong Daughter

- Don't disclose too much personal information when first dating.
- Don't compete with other women when on a date.
- Don't text or talk on the phone when on a date.
- Don't leave your drink unattended.
- Don't go to an isolated location.
- Don't go home with him, or invite him inside your home.
- Don't violate your values and ground rules.
- Don't have sex before you are ready.
- Don't stay in a situation where you feel

uncomfortable; it only gets worse.

## Safety Strategies While on a Date

- Stay in a public place during initial dates
- Find out more about your date.
- Watch your date's reactions for changes in demeanor and inattentiveness.
- Be attentive to what is happening around you.
- Be cautious of his sudden change in plans.
- Be assertive and sincere about your sexual comfort level when dating.

106

- Break away from an uncomfortable situation.
- Be aware of set ups for assault and exploitation.
- Introduce your date to different friends and family, and ask for their feedback.
- In between dates, assess his actions

## Raise Your Daughter to be Aware of the Dangers of Consensual Isolation

Teach her to be wary of going to isolated locations with someone she just met or is acquainted with. Robbery, burglary, kidnapping, and rape can occur in these circumstances.

To avoid consensual isolation, have your daughter insist that she remain in public venues when dating or getting to know someone.

Going to a secluded location with a boy or someone on a date, carries different meanings and expectations.

This is a difficult one to get across to a daughter who is enamored of her date so provide her with smart options:

- Enable her GPS tracking
- Make sure she calls back once in a while during a date.
- Tell her to keep her cell phone on her. Instruct her to

go to the bathroom when inside a residence or flee, using her phone to call for help.
- Teach her to be aware of her surroundings and to take in details.
- Teach her that it is better to get to know her date first without going to an isolated place before she starts dating him.

# Protecting A Young Daughter

One of the best shields against child abduction is to educate yourself on a predator's tricks in getting a child to trust them and to follow them.

Teach and make your child beware of strangers, acquaintances' strange behavior, boundaries and limits on who to trust, and how to get help.

And this is a given: Never leave your child alone.

## Personal Safety

Statistically, single women are the most prone to being attacked.

We covered the aspects of safety, learning to fight, and how to be keenly aware to be a tougher target in the chapters before.

110

# College Safety Tips

College women are very vulnerable, especially their first year of college.

Teaching your daughter all the self-defense techniques will help her be a tougher target no matter whether she is in high school, college, married with children.

# Conclusion

Knowing the basics of safety and protection as a person, whether it is for your daughter, wife, sister, mother, sons, or even for yourself is empowering and strong.

Taking responsibility for your own safety and knowing you can do your best to protect and strengthen yourself is one of the best way to prepare yourself and your loved ones on their journey through life.

# About the Authors

Co-writing this book on Raising strong girls are multi-award-winning author Kailin Gow, who is well-known for writing strong women characters in her fiction books, author of Strong, and also the co-host and producer of the Kailin Gow's Go Girl Travel and Lost History TV Series on Amazon, who features women leaders and innovators; and her husband, attorney Finlay Gow, who is an Employment/HR and Corporate Attorney who has worked on Harassment cases, is a father of a strong daughter, and has a woman General as an ancestor.

Together in Raising Strong Daughters, they tackle the topics on Raising

a Girl with Self-esteem, Raising a Girl to be
Aware of Harassment issues, Raising a Girl
who knows how to Defend Herself, and
more!

# More Food and Lifestyle Books

If you enjoyed Raising A Strong Daughter: What Fathers Should Know, then pick up other Kailin Gow's Non-Fiction Food, Lifestyle, and Self-Improvement Books.

Now Available Here:

## Kailin Gow's Go Girl Guide to SUPERFOODS

Based on the hit TV Series about food, travel, and lost history, hosted by Kailin Gow, comes this guide to Superfoods and recipes that any busy on-the-go person can make to create a healthier, energized, and good-for-you delicious meal.

# The Loving Summer Cookbook

A cookbook with recipes for healthy meals that are easy to prepare, heart-happy, low glycemic, and low caloried.

# About the Author

Kailin Gow is the author of over 400 books, some of which have won awards. A former executive for large corporations, she had the chance to travel the world. Now she's a full-time author, award-winning filmmaker, producer, and television personality pursuing her dreams to help people live fuller and better.